This journal belongs to

_____

In honor of

_____

# The First 28

A Black Woman's Journal For Surviving
The First 28 Days of Losing Her Spouse

Margo Thomas

Junk@noo Consulting LLC
www.junkanoopublications.com
Valdosta, GA 31605
229-234-2306

Printed in the United States of America

ISBN: 979-8-9859839-5-1

Images: Canva.com; iStock

## Introduction

Losing a spouse is a horrific experience. There is no way to prepare for the heartache and pain that comes when you lose the love of your life. There are so many emotions attached to grief - sorrow, despair, pain, and even anger. The rollercoaster of this new life can be too much to bear at times. It may seem as if you are all alone and no one else truly understands what you're going through.

Sometimes, as black women, we feel pressured to be strong, even in our grief. We are taught over our lifetime to always be the one everyone else comes to for help. We wear the "strong" title as a badge of honor. We usually put on our capes and try to save everyone else. I'll tell you that this is not the time to be Wonder Woman. Lean on your support system for help, especially during the *first 28 days after losing your spouse.*

My husband lost his battle with cancer a week before my birthday. At that time, he had completed two rounds of chemo and one radiation treatment. His last scan gave us some hope as we began preparing for a stem cell transplant. During the preliminary tests, we learned about a new tumor, which had aggressively spread to his brain. Some tough decisions had to be made in a short span of time. We prayed that God would perform a miracle on our behalf, but unfortunately, God had other plans.

The journey through grief can be long and arduous. Your emotions become like waves on the ocean. One moment, you are fine and another moment, you are not. In one second, you can be smiling at a memory and within seconds, the wave of tears can knock you off your feet.  I hate to say it, but the first 28 days will feel like hell! There are lots of decisions to be made - preparing for a memorial or funeral, communicating with life insurance companies, banks, the Social Security office, working through family dynamics, and so much more. It can be overwhelming, especially if you are doing it all alone. As I've said before, lean on your support system.

Many will ask what you need and honestly, you may not know what you need in the moment. Most people will not push you because they won't know how you'll react. Yes, this is new territory for you, but it is also new for well-meaning friends and family. Don't be afraid to ask for help when you figure out what you need. I'll also add that whatever you ask for may not be done exactly as you would like it to be done. Relax. Breathe. The dishes may not be arranged in the dishwasher the way you prefer, but you just need them cleaned, right? Don't alienate that person by fighting over something as trivial as this. You have bigger battles to fight moving forward.

Your support system may not only include family and friends. I also relied on my church family, my counselor (not a grief counselor), my doctor, a local grief group, and most importantly, my relationship with God. I am grateful that I have a strong support system. Sadly though, I recognize that some may not have that. If you know that your family and friends will not help you, I encourage you to seek help from somewhere else. While you may be able to go through this journey alone, isolation often does not provide a positive outcome. Unfortunately, the usual outcome of isolation often results in an unhealthy dependence on 'things' that harm us rather than help us heal - i.e. drugs, alcohol, excessive shopping, constant movement; anything to muffle the thoughts going on in your head.

My hope is that this journal will help you discover positive ways to get through the next 28 days of your grief journey. Each day will allow you to explore your thoughts and feelings in the morning when you awake and, in the evening before you go to bed. At the end of each week, you will have an opportunity to write a love letter to your spouse. Be open with your feelings. Let your spouse know what you wish you could have said. I can't promise that this will be easy. The first time I did this exercise, I cried, and cried, and cried some more. At the end of it, I felt better. I got to release my emotions while expressing my true inner thoughts and feelings, so I believe it was worth every tear.

The journey through grief has its twist and turns. Because of that, I figured I you would need a few tools in your bag to help you push through, especially on the days when you don't feel like it. The overarching themes of this journal are comfort, strength, peace, and hope.

I wish you all the best as you navigate this new life without your spouse and I pray that God gives you comfort, strength, peace, and hope as you find your own way to navigate through this journey.

Blessings,

# Week 1

# Comfort

"When the Lord saw her, His heart overflowed with compassion. "Don't cry! he said" (Luke 7:13 NLV)

## Thought for the week:

Comfort ~ "When the Lord saw her, His heart overflowed with compassion. "Don't cry! he said" (Luke 7:13 NLV)

The Oxford dictionary defines Comfort as, "The easing or alleviation of a person's feelings of grief or distress." It is difficult to find comfort when grieving a spouse. There are too many daily 'in-your-face' moments. Honestly though, the first few weeks you will probably be a little numb, especially if your spouse's death was unexpected. Each of our journey through this grief is individualized. What may work for me, may or may not work for someone else and vice-versa. For me, it was comforting to be around family and friends sharing our fondest memories of my husband and sometimes laughing at some of those memories. There is a saying that laughter is the greatest medicine. This held true for me during some of the toughest moments. I know that we are not all followers of Christ and I don't mean to sound 'churchy', but I would be remiss if I did not acknowledge that I gained great comfort through my relationship with God. I believe reading the Bible and reciting God's word comforted me in ways I cannot express. If reading the Bible is not your thing, then find inspirational quotes to help you get through this. I strongly believe we have to do what we have to do to survive.

I hope that somehow you will find comfort this week to help ease the excruciating pain you may be feeling at this moment. Be open and please don't give up. Be strong for YOU.

# Morning check in

DATE _____

AT THIS MOMENT, I FEEL

I'M AFRAID THAT
_____

ONE THING I CAN DO TO GET
THROUGH THE DAY

○
_____

THREE THINGS I NEED TO GET
DONE (E.G., CALL ABOUT SS
BENEFITS)
_____

THE MEMORY I WILL FOCUS ON
TODAY IS
_____

I WILL ASK THESE PEOPLE FOR
HELP TODAY
_____

IF YOU WERE HERE, I BELIEVE YOU
WOULD TELL ME TO
_____

THOUGHT FOR THE WEEK
_____

*"WHEN THE LORD SAW HER, HIS
HEART OVERFLOWED WITH
COMPASSION. "DON'T CRY! HE SAID"
(LUKE 7:13 NLV)*

# Evening check in

AT THIS MOMENT, I FEEL

THE HARDEST TIME OF THE DAY
TODAY WAS

I THOUGHT OF YOU  TODAY WHEN

MY GREATEST TRIGGER TODAY
WAS

I FOUND HOPE TODAY WHEN

IF I COULD TALK TO YOU RIGHT
NOW, I WOULD TELL YOU

I CELEBRATED YOU TODAY BY

# Morning check in

DATE _____

AT THIS MOMENT, I FEEL

I'M AFRAID THAT
_____

ONE THING I CAN DO TO GET
THROUGH THE DAY

○
_____

THREE THINGS I NEED TO GET
DONE (E.G., CALL ABOUT SS
BENEFITS)
_____

THE MEMORY I WILL FOCUS ON
TODAY IS
_____

I WILL ASK THESE PEOPLE FOR
HELP TODAY
_____

IF YOU WERE HERE, I BELIEVE YOU
WOULD TELL ME TO
_____

THOUGHT FOR THE WEEK
_____

*"WHEN THE LORD SAW HER, HIS
HEART OVERFLOWED WITH
COMPASSION. "DON'T CRY! HE SAID"
(LUKE 7:13 NLV)*

# Evening check in

AT THIS MOMENT, I FEEL

THE HARDEST TIME OF THE DAY
TODAY WAS
_____

I THOUGHT OF YOU  TODAY WHEN
_____

MY GREATEST TRIGGER TODAY
WAS
_____

I FOUND HOPE TODAY WHEN
_____

IF I COULD TALK TO YOU RIGHT
NOW, I WOULD TELL YOU
_____

I CELEBRATED YOU TODAY BY

# Morning check in

DATE _____

AT THIS MOMENT, I FEEL

I'M AFRAID THAT
_____

ONE THING I CAN DO TO GET THROUGH THE DAY

○ _____

THREE THINGS I NEED TO GET DONE (E.G., CALL ABOUT SS BENEFITS)
_____

THE MEMORY I WILL FOCUS ON TODAY IS
_____

I WILL ASK THESE PEOPLE FOR HELP TODAY
_____

IF YOU WERE HERE, I BELIEVE YOU WOULD TELL ME TO
_____

THOUGHT FOR THE WEEK
_____

*"WHEN THE LORD SAW HER, HIS HEART OVERFLOWED WITH COMPASSION. "DON'T CRY! HE SAID" (LUKE 7:13 NLV)*

# Evening check in

AT THIS MOMENT, I FEEL

I THOUGHT OF YOU TODAY WHEN

I FOUND HOPE TODAY WHEN

I CELEBRATED YOU TODAY BY

THE HARDEST TIME OF THE DAY
TODAY WAS

MY GREATEST TRIGGER TODAY
WAS

IF I COULD TALK TO YOU RIGHT
NOW, I WOULD TELL YOU

# Morning check in

DATE _____

AT THIS MOMENT, I FEEL

ONE THING I CAN DO TO GET THROUGH THE DAY

○ _____

THE MEMORY I WILL FOCUS ON TODAY IS
_____

IF YOU WERE HERE, I BELIEVE YOU WOULD TELL ME TO
_____

I'M AFRAID THAT
_____

THREE THINGS I NEED TO GET DONE (E.G., CALL ABOUT SS BENEFITS)
_____

I WILL ASK THESE PEOPLE FOR HELP TODAY
_____

THOUGHT FOR THE WEEK
_____

*"WHEN THE LORD SAW HER, HIS HEART OVERFLOWED WITH COMPASSION. "DON'T CRY! HE SAID" (LUKE 7:13 NLV)*

# Evening check in

AT THIS MOMENT, I FEEL

THE HARDEST TIME OF THE DAY
TODAY WAS
_____

I THOUGHT OF YOU  TODAY WHEN
_____

MY GREATEST TRIGGER TODAY
WAS
_____

I FOUND HOPE TODAY WHEN
_____

IF I COULD TALK TO YOU RIGHT
NOW, I WOULD TELL YOU
_____

I CELEBRATED YOU TODAY BY

# Morning check in

DATE _____

AT THIS MOMENT, I FEEL

ONE THING I CAN DO TO GET THROUGH THE DAY

○ _____

THE MEMORY I WILL FOCUS ON TODAY IS
_____

IF YOU WERE HERE, I BELIEVE YOU WOULD TELL ME TO
_____

I'M AFRAID THAT
_____

THREE THINGS I NEED TO GET DONE (E.G., CALL ABOUT SS BENEFITS)
_____

I WILL ASK THESE PEOPLE FOR HELP TODAY
_____

THOUGHT FOR THE WEEK
_____

*"WHEN THE LORD SAW HER, HIS HEART OVERFLOWED WITH COMPASSION. "DON'T CRY! HE SAID" (LUKE 7:13 NLV)*

# Evening check in

AT THIS MOMENT, I FEEL

THE HARDEST TIME OF THE DAY
TODAY WAS

I THOUGHT OF YOU  TODAY WHEN

MY GREATEST TRIGGER TODAY
WAS

I FOUND HOPE TODAY WHEN

IF I COULD TALK TO YOU RIGHT
NOW, I WOULD TELL YOU

I CELEBRATED YOU TODAY BY

# Morning check in

DATE _____

AT THIS MOMENT, I FEEL

ONE THING I CAN DO TO GET
THROUGH THE DAY

○  _____

THE MEMORY I WILL FOCUS ON
TODAY IS
_____

IF YOU WERE HERE, I BELIEVE YOU
WOULD TELL ME TO
_____

I'M AFRAID THAT
_____

THREE THINGS I NEED TO GET
DONE (E.G., CALL ABOUT SS
BENEFITS)
_____

I WILL ASK THESE PEOPLE FOR
HELP TODAY
_____

THOUGHT FOR THE WEEK
_____

*"WHEN THE LORD SAW HER, HIS
HEART OVERFLOWED WITH
COMPASSION. "DON'T CRY! HE SAID"
(LUKE 7:13 NLV)*

# Evening check in

AT THIS MOMENT, I FEEL

I THOUGHT OF YOU  TODAY WHEN
_____

I FOUND HOPE TODAY WHEN
_____

I CELEBRATED YOU TODAY BY

THE HARDEST TIME OF THE DAY
TODAY WAS
_____

MY GREATEST TRIGGER TODAY
WAS
_____

IF I COULD TALK TO YOU RIGHT
NOW, I WOULD TELL YOU
_____

# Morning check in

DATE _____

AT THIS MOMENT, I FEEL

ONE THING I CAN DO TO GET THROUGH THE DAY

○ _____

THE MEMORY I WILL FOCUS ON TODAY IS
_____

IF YOU WERE HERE, I BELIEVE YOU WOULD TELL ME TO
_____

I'M AFRAID THAT
_____

THREE THINGS I NEED TO GET DONE (E.G., CALL ABOUT SS BENEFITS)
_____

I WILL ASK THESE PEOPLE FOR HELP TODAY
_____

THOUGHT FOR THE WEEK
_____

*"WHEN THE LORD SAW HER, HIS HEART OVERFLOWED WITH COMPASSION. "DON'T CRY! HE SAID"*
*(LUKE 7:13 NLV)*

# Evening check in

AT THIS MOMENT, I FEEL

THE HARDEST TIME OF THE DAY
TODAY WAS

I THOUGHT OF YOU TODAY WHEN

MY GREATEST TRIGGER TODAY
WAS

I FOUND HOPE TODAY WHEN

IF I COULD TALK TO YOU RIGHT
NOW, I WOULD TELL YOU

I CELEBRATED YOU TODAY BY

### *Prompts for writing a love letter to your spouse*

I'm sure this week was not easy. If you're like me, you are going to miss sharing little things with your spouse. I remember picking up the phone to call or text him about something I heard or had seen in my daily travels, only to remember that I can't do that anymore. At some point, I had to find alternative ways to share my thoughts with him. While I still speak them out loud, some days it's better for me to write them down. Who knows what can happen when we put pen to paper, right?

So, here is what I want you to do. Don't overthink this exercise. You have been writing your thoughts all week. You can put some of those thoughts together to create a letter to your spouse. To help make this as simple as possible, I'll leave some of the weekly prompts below. Go through your responses to the daily check-ins and write whatever feels right to you.

- This week, my biggest fear was.......
- The most difficult time of the day for me this week was......
- I thought of you when........
- My fondest memory of you this week was......
- I got these things done this week....
- I found hope this week when.....
- If I could talk to you right now, I would tell you....
- I believe you would tell me to.....

Maybe there is something else you prefer to share with your spouse. This is strictly about you. Do whatever works for you.

Date _____

*Dear*

_____

_____

_____

_____

_____

_____

_____

_____

_____

_____

_____

_____

_____

_____

_____

_____

_____

_____

_____

_____

## *A Photographic Tribute to Your Spouse*

One of the things that got me through each week was seeing pictures of my husband and I together with family and friends. Some pictures captured us at home, while others captured us during our travels. Some pictures were staged and serious, and others were just us - being goofy. During one of the weekly group-sessions I attended at a local church, we were asked to bring a photo that represented our loved one. Because I had been looking at pictures each day, I knew exactly which picture I should take. Yes, I took a goofy one! We all shared our photos, as well as the story behind them. Interestingly enough, we all chose fun or funny memories attached to the pictures we chose.

While the first few months are difficult to navigate, good memories will help you through the process. Find one picture or make a collage of pictures that can give you some comfort for the week ahead. This picture can be one of your spouse or any picture(s) you choose. Just attach it here.

# Week 2

# Strength

"Someday your pain will become the source of your strength. Face it. Brave it. You will make it" ~ Dodinsky

**Thought for the week:**

*"Someday your pain will become the source of your strength. Face it. Brave it. You will make it". ~ Dodinsky*

Recently, a friend told me that I didn't need to be strong for everyone else. My response was that I wasn't trying to be strong for anyone else. I was trying to be strong for me. I understood that while falling apart may have felt justified, I did not want to be so overcome by grief that I could not shake it off. As black women, we are taught to be strong for everyone else, sometimes to the detriment of our own well-being. I had to maintain my strength while my husband was battling cancer because I knew he needed me to be strong then. However, I can honestly say that it was not a false bravado. My friends and family were praying for my strength. I was praying for my strength. Whenever I was asked what I needed, I usually thought , 'I need strength just to function today.' I am sure God gave me the strength I needed, especially to get through the first few months.

Prior to my husband's death, I had been meeting regularly with a counselor. We were working on different ways to cope with being a caregiver. So, while death was not the outcome I was expecting, when my husband passed, I was already in the process of figuring out how to function. I believe this helped me to be stronger in the moment because I was subconsciously prepared for the 'what-if'.

Maybe that is not your story and you cannot figure out how to be strong for yourself. If you are a person of faith, I strongly suggest that you ask God to give you strength to get through each day. If you are not a person of faith, consider reading books or listening to podcasts about grief and surviving the loss of a spouse. Speak with your doctor and find a counselor or grief group to help you navigate this process. I found a quote that says, "Strong people still need their hands held." [author unknown]

I believe this is one journey we don't want to take alone. It is better to have someone hold us up during the times when we are falling apart.

The goal is to get you to take one step and then another, even if they are slow and deliberate. Eventually your steps will get a little faster, but remember, there is no rush. You are doing this at your own pace - a pace that is comfortable for you.

# Morning check in

AT THIS MOMENT, I FEEL

ONE THING I CAN DO TO GET THROUGH THE DAY

○ _____

THE MEMORY I WILL FOCUS ON TODAY IS
_____

IF YOU WERE HERE, I BELIEVE YOU WOULD TELL ME TO
_____

I'M AFRAID THAT
_____

THREE THINGS I NEED TO GET DONE (E.G., CALL ABOUT SS BENEFITS)
_____

I WILL ASK THESE PEOPLE FOR HELP TODAY
_____

THOUGHT FOR THE WEEK
_____

*"WHEN THE LORD SAW HER, HIS HEART OVERFLOWED WITH COMPASSION. "DON'T CRY! HE SAID" (LUKE 7:13 NLV)*

# Evening check in

AT THIS MOMENT, I FEEL

I THOUGHT OF YOU  TODAY WHEN

I FOUND HOPE TODAY WHEN

I CELEBRATED YOU TODAY BY

THE HARDEST TIME OF THE DAY
TODAY WAS

MY GREATEST TRIGGER TODAY
WAS

IF I COULD TALK TO YOU RIGHT
NOW, I WOULD TELL YOU

# Morning check in

DATE _____

AT THIS MOMENT, I FEEL

ONE THING I CAN DO TO GET
THROUGH THE DAY

○ _____

THE MEMORY I WILL FOCUS ON
TODAY IS
_____

IF YOU WERE HERE, I BELIEVE YOU
WOULD TELL ME TO
_____

I'M AFRAID THAT
_____

THREE THINGS I NEED TO GET
DONE (E.G., CALL ABOUT SS
BENEFITS)
_____

I WILL ASK THESE PEOPLE FOR
HELP TODAY
_____

THOUGHT FOR THE WEEK
_____

*"WHEN THE LORD SAW HER, HIS
HEART OVERFLOWED WITH
COMPASSION. "DON'T CRY! HE SAID"
(LUKE 7:13 NLV)*

# Evening check in

AT THIS MOMENT, I FEEL

I THOUGHT OF YOU  TODAY WHEN
_____

I FOUND HOPE TODAY WHEN
_____

I CELEBRATED YOU TODAY BY

THE HARDEST TIME OF THE DAY
TODAY WAS
_____

MY GREATEST TRIGGER TODAY
WAS
_____

IF I COULD TALK TO YOU RIGHT
NOW, I WOULD TELL YOU
_____

# Morning check in

DATE _____

AT THIS MOMENT, I FEEL

I'M AFRAID THAT
_____

THREE THINGS I NEED TO GET DONE (E.G., CALL ABOUT SS BENEFITS)
_____

ONE THING I CAN DO TO GET THROUGH THE DAY

○ _____

THE MEMORY I WILL FOCUS ON TODAY IS
_____

I WILL ASK THESE PEOPLE FOR HELP TODAY
_____

IF YOU WERE HERE, I BELIEVE YOU WOULD TELL ME TO
_____

THOUGHT FOR THE WEEK
_____

*"WHEN THE LORD SAW HER, HIS HEART OVERFLOWED WITH COMPASSION. "DON'T CRY! HE SAID"*
*(LUKE 7:13 NLV)*

# Evening check in

AT THIS MOMENT, I FEEL

THE HARDEST TIME OF THE DAY
TODAY WAS
_____

I THOUGHT OF YOU  TODAY WHEN
_____

MY GREATEST TRIGGER TODAY
WAS
_____

I FOUND HOPE TODAY WHEN
_____

IF I COULD TALK TO YOU RIGHT
NOW, I WOULD TELL YOU
_____

I CELEBRATED YOU TODAY BY

# Morning check in

DATE _____

AT THIS MOMENT, I FEEL

ONE THING I CAN DO TO GET
THROUGH THE DAY

○ _____

THE MEMORY I WILL FOCUS ON
TODAY IS
_____

IF YOU WERE HERE, I BELIEVE YOU
WOULD TELL ME TO
_____

I'M AFRAID THAT
_____

THREE THINGS I NEED TO GET
DONE (E.G., CALL ABOUT SS
BENEFITS)
_____

I WILL ASK THESE PEOPLE FOR
HELP TODAY
_____

THOUGHT FOR THE WEEK
_____

*"WHEN THE LORD SAW HER, HIS
HEART OVERFLOWED WITH
COMPASSION. "DON'T CRY! HE SAID"
(LUKE 7:13 NLV)*

# Evening check in

AT THIS MOMENT, I FEEL

I THOUGHT OF YOU TODAY WHEN
_____

I FOUND HOPE TODAY WHEN
_____

I CELEBRATED YOU TODAY BY

THE HARDEST TIME OF THE DAY TODAY WAS
_____

MY GREATEST TRIGGER TODAY WAS
_____

IF I COULD TALK TO YOU RIGHT NOW, I WOULD TELL YOU
_____

# Morning check in

AT THIS MOMENT, I FEEL

ONE THING I CAN DO TO GET
THROUGH THE DAY

○ _____

THE MEMORY I WILL FOCUS ON
TODAY IS
_____

IF YOU WERE HERE, I BELIEVE YOU
WOULD TELL ME TO
_____

I'M AFRAID THAT
_____

THREE THINGS I NEED TO GET
DONE (E.G., CALL ABOUT SS
BENEFITS)
_____

I WILL ASK THESE PEOPLE FOR
HELP TODAY
_____

THOUGHT FOR THE WEEK
_____

*"WHEN THE LORD SAW HER, HIS
HEART OVERFLOWED WITH
COMPASSION. "DON'T CRY! HE SAID"
(LUKE 7:13 NLV)*

# Evening check in

AT THIS MOMENT, I FEEL

I THOUGHT OF YOU  TODAY WHEN
_____

I FOUND HOPE TODAY WHEN
_____

I CELEBRATED YOU TODAY BY

THE HARDEST TIME OF THE DAY
TODAY WAS
_____

MY GREATEST TRIGGER TODAY
WAS
_____

IF I COULD TALK TO YOU RIGHT
NOW, I WOULD TELL YOU
_____

# Morning check in

DATE _____

AT THIS MOMENT, I FEEL

I'M AFRAID THAT
_____

ONE THING I CAN DO TO GET THROUGH THE DAY

○ _____

THREE THINGS I NEED TO GET DONE (E.G., CALL ABOUT SS BENEFITS)
_____

THE MEMORY I WILL FOCUS ON TODAY IS
_____

I WILL ASK THESE PEOPLE FOR HELP TODAY
_____

IF YOU WERE HERE, I BELIEVE YOU WOULD TELL ME TO
_____

THOUGHT FOR THE WEEK
_____

*"WHEN THE LORD SAW HER, HIS HEART OVERFLOWED WITH COMPASSION. "DON'T CRY! HE SAID"
(LUKE 7:13 NLV)*

# Evening check in

AT THIS MOMENT, I FEEL

THE HARDEST TIME OF THE DAY
TODAY WAS

I THOUGHT OF YOU  TODAY WHEN

MY GREATEST TRIGGER TODAY
WAS

I FOUND HOPE TODAY WHEN

IF I COULD TALK TO YOU RIGHT
NOW, I WOULD TELL YOU

I CELEBRATED YOU TODAY BY

# Morning check in

DATE _____

AT THIS MOMENT, I FEEL

I'M AFRAID THAT
_____

THREE THINGS I NEED TO GET
DONE (E.G., CALL ABOUT SS
BENEFITS)
_____

ONE THING I CAN DO TO GET
THROUGH THE DAY

○ _____

THE MEMORY I WILL FOCUS ON
TODAY IS
_____

I WILL ASK THESE PEOPLE FOR
HELP TODAY
_____

IF YOU WERE HERE, I BELIEVE YOU
WOULD TELL ME TO
_____

THOUGHT FOR THE WEEK
_____

*"WHEN THE LORD SAW HER, HIS
HEART OVERFLOWED WITH
COMPASSION. "DON'T CRY! HE SAID"
(LUKE 7:13 NLV)*

# Evening check in

AT THIS MOMENT, I FEEL

I THOUGHT OF YOU  TODAY WHEN

I FOUND HOPE TODAY WHEN

I CELEBRATED YOU TODAY BY

THE HARDEST TIME OF THE DAY
TODAY WAS

MY GREATEST TRIGGER TODAY
WAS

IF I COULD TALK TO YOU RIGHT
NOW, I WOULD TELL YOU

## Prompts for writing a love letter to your spouse

You've completed another week. I'm sure it still seems unreal. How are you feeling? Can you think of one thing that happened recently that made you feel a little stronger? It doesn't have to be anything earth shattering. Maybe you went back to work and you didn't fall apart at the staff meeting. That's a big deal, Sis! Take that as a win. Maybe your win was something seemingly smaller, like getting out of bed and taking a shower, which helped you prepare mentally for the day. I'll take that as a win as well.

This is the time to write your letter to your spouse. Again, don't overthink this exercise. Use some of your thoughts from this week's check-in, or not. The weekly prompts are below. Go through your responses to the daily check-ins and write whatever feels right to you.

- This week, my biggest fear was.......
- The most difficult time f the day for me this week was......
- I thought of you when........
- My fondest memory of you this week was......
- I got these things done this week....
- I found hope this week when.....
- If I could talk to you right now, I would tell you....
- I believe you would tell me to.....

If you have something else you prefer to share with your spouse, go for it.

Date _____

*Dear*

_____
_____
_____
_____
_____
_____
_____
_____
_____
_____
_____
_____
_____
_____
_____
_____
_____
_____

### *A Photographic Tribute To Your Spouse*

Choose another picture or create a collage of pictures you believe will make you feel stronger for the week ahead.

# Week 3

# Peace

"Do not worry about anything; instead pray about everything. Tell God what you need; and thank Him for all He has done. Then you will experience God's peace, which exceeds anything we can understand." (Phill 4:6-7 NLV)

## *Thought for the week*

Peace ~ "Do not worry about anything; instead pray about everything. Tell God what you need; and thank Him for all He has done. Then you will experience God's peace, which exceeds anything we can understand. His peace will guard your hearts and minds as you live in Christ Jesus." (Phill 4:6-7 NLV)

Early one morning, I woke up feeling extremely anxious. I immediately picked up my cell phone, opened the calculator app and started calculating. I have a degree in accounting and I've worked with budgets for many years. If you know anything about personality tests, you may recognize that most accountants and finance professionals are usually very analytical. Simply put, we like to figure things out - we are often very good at overthinking things as well. So, when I woke up that morning, I was trying to figure out how I would make the money I had work for me. I understood that, not only did I lose my husband, but I also lost a significant part of my income. As I calculated the different scenarios, I felt my heart rate speed up. It seemed as if I was having a mini-panic attack (I've never had one before, but I imagine that is how people feel when they have an anxiety attack). In the midst of it, I heard a small voice whisper, "Say a scripture". The Bible verse that came to mind in that moment was, "Peace. Be still" (Mark 4:39). I felt a peace that I couldn't really understand, but I welcomed it and I immediately fell asleep. Since then, I haven't experienced that level of anxiety, thankfully.

By now, you are more than likely overwhelmed by the major changes in your life. It is possible that you are afraid that you won't get over this feeling of fear. I get it. You are in a difficult position, but if you allow your fear to take over your life completely, you can drown in your grief to the point where you don't want to live.

I am not saying don't grieve your spouse and I'm not telling you how long to grieve your spouse. It's a personal journey. However, I hope that at some point you will receive a sense of peace that will help you to weather this storm. I found that peace through my relationship with God. You will need to determine what gives you peace (not what numbs you) and once you find it, lean into it daily.

# Morning check in

DATE _____

AT THIS MOMENT, I FEEL

I'M AFRAID THAT
_____

ONE THING I CAN DO TO GET
THROUGH THE DAY

○ _____

THREE THINGS I NEED TO GET
DONE (E.G., CALL ABOUT SS
BENEFITS)
_____

THE MEMORY I WILL FOCUS ON
TODAY IS
_____

I WILL ASK THESE PEOPLE FOR
HELP TODAY
_____

IF YOU WERE HERE, I BELIEVE YOU
WOULD TELL ME TO
_____

THOUGHT FOR THE WEEK
_____

*"WHEN THE LORD SAW HER, HIS
HEART OVERFLOWED WITH
COMPASSION. "DON'T CRY! HE SAID"
(LUKE 7:13 NLV)*

# Evening check in

AT THIS MOMENT, I FEEL

I THOUGHT OF YOU  TODAY WHEN

I FOUND HOPE TODAY WHEN

I CELEBRATED YOU TODAY BY

THE HARDEST TIME OF THE DAY TODAY WAS

MY GREATEST TRIGGER TODAY WAS

IF I COULD TALK TO YOU RIGHT NOW, I WOULD TELL YOU

# Morning check in

DATE _____

AT THIS MOMENT, I FEEL

I'M AFRAID THAT
_____

ONE THING I CAN DO TO GET
THROUGH THE DAY

○ _____

THREE THINGS I NEED TO GET
DONE (E.G., CALL ABOUT SS
BENEFITS)
_____

THE MEMORY I WILL FOCUS ON
TODAY IS
_____

I WILL ASK THESE PEOPLE FOR
HELP TODAY
_____

IF YOU WERE HERE, I BELIEVE YOU
WOULD TELL ME TO
_____

THOUGHT FOR THE WEEK
_____

*"WHEN THE LORD SAW HER, HIS
HEART OVERFLOWED WITH
COMPASSION. "DON'T CRY! HE SAID"
(LUKE 7:13 NLV)*

# Evening check in

AT THIS MOMENT, I FEEL

I THOUGHT OF YOU  TODAY WHEN

I FOUND HOPE TODAY WHEN

I CELEBRATED YOU TODAY BY

THE HARDEST TIME OF THE DAY
TODAY WAS

MY GREATEST TRIGGER TODAY
WAS

IF I COULD TALK TO YOU RIGHT
NOW, I WOULD TELL YOU

# Morning check in

DATE _____

AT THIS MOMENT, I FEEL

I'M AFRAID THAT
_____

ONE THING I CAN DO TO GET
THROUGH THE DAY

○ _____

THREE THINGS I NEED TO GET
DONE (E.G., CALL ABOUT SS
BENEFITS)
_____

THE MEMORY I WILL FOCUS ON
TODAY IS
_____

I WILL ASK THESE PEOPLE FOR
HELP TODAY
_____

IF YOU WERE HERE, I BELIEVE YOU
WOULD TELL ME TO
_____

THOUGHT FOR THE WEEK
_____

*"WHEN THE LORD SAW HER, HIS
HEART OVERFLOWED WITH
COMPASSION. "DON'T CRY! HE SAID"
(LUKE 7:13 NLV)*

# Evening check in

AT THIS MOMENT, I FEEL

I THOUGHT OF YOU TODAY WHEN

I FOUND HOPE TODAY WHEN

I CELEBRATED YOU TODAY BY

THE HARDEST TIME OF THE DAY
TODAY WAS

MY GREATEST TRIGGER TODAY
WAS

IF I COULD TALK TO YOU RIGHT
NOW, I WOULD TELL YOU

# Morning check in

DATE _____

AT THIS MOMENT, I FEEL

ONE THING I CAN DO TO GET
THROUGH THE DAY

○ _____

THE MEMORY I WILL FOCUS ON
TODAY IS
_____

IF YOU WERE HERE, I BELIEVE YOU
WOULD TELL ME TO
_____

I'M AFRAID THAT
_____

THREE THINGS I NEED TO GET
DONE (E.G., CALL ABOUT SS
BENEFITS)
_____

I WILL ASK THESE PEOPLE FOR
HELP TODAY
_____

THOUGHT FOR THE WEEK
_____

*"WHEN THE LORD SAW HER, HIS
HEART OVERFLOWED WITH
COMPASSION. "DON'T CRY! HE SAID"
(LUKE 7:13 NLV)*

# Evening check in

AT THIS MOMENT, I FEEL

I THOUGHT OF YOU  TODAY WHEN

I FOUND HOPE TODAY WHEN

I CELEBRATED YOU TODAY BY

THE HARDEST TIME OF THE DAY TODAY WAS

MY GREATEST TRIGGER TODAY WAS

IF I COULD TALK TO YOU RIGHT NOW, I WOULD TELL YOU

# Morning check in

DATE _____

AT THIS MOMENT, I FEEL

ONE THING I CAN DO TO GET THROUGH THE DAY

○ _____

THE MEMORY I WILL FOCUS ON TODAY IS
_____

IF YOU WERE HERE, I BELIEVE YOU WOULD TELL ME TO
_____

I'M AFRAID THAT
_____

THREE THINGS I NEED TO GET DONE (E.G., CALL ABOUT SS BENEFITS)
_____

I WILL ASK THESE PEOPLE FOR HELP TODAY
_____

THOUGHT FOR THE WEEK
_____

*"WHEN THE LORD SAW HER, HIS HEART OVERFLOWED WITH COMPASSION. "DON'T CRY! HE SAID" (LUKE 7:13 NLV)*

# Evening check in

AT THIS MOMENT, I FEEL

I THOUGHT OF YOU TODAY WHEN

I FOUND HOPE TODAY WHEN

I CELEBRATED YOU TODAY BY

THE HARDEST TIME OF THE DAY TODAY WAS

MY GREATEST TRIGGER TODAY WAS

IF I COULD TALK TO YOU RIGHT NOW, I WOULD TELL YOU

# Morning check in

DATE _____

AT THIS MOMENT, I FEEL

I'M AFRAID THAT
_____

THREE THINGS I NEED TO GET
DONE (E.G., CALL ABOUT SS
BENEFITS)
_____

ONE THING I CAN DO TO GET
THROUGH THE DAY

○ _____

THE MEMORY I WILL FOCUS ON
TODAY IS
_____

I WILL ASK THESE PEOPLE FOR
HELP TODAY
_____

IF YOU WERE HERE, I BELIEVE YOU
WOULD TELL ME TO
_____

THOUGHT FOR THE WEEK
_____

*"WHEN THE LORD SAW HER, HIS
HEART OVERFLOWED WITH
COMPASSION. "DON'T CRY! HE SAID"
(LUKE 7:13 NLV)*

# Evening check in

AT THIS MOMENT, I FEEL

I THOUGHT OF YOU  TODAY WHEN

I FOUND HOPE TODAY WHEN

I CELEBRATED YOU TODAY BY

THE HARDEST TIME OF THE DAY
TODAY WAS

MY GREATEST TRIGGER TODAY
WAS

IF I COULD TALK TO YOU RIGHT
NOW, I WOULD TELL YOU

# Morning check in

DATE _____

AT THIS MOMENT, I FEEL

ONE THING I CAN DO TO GET
THROUGH THE DAY

○ _____

THE MEMORY I WILL FOCUS ON
TODAY IS
_____

IF YOU WERE HERE, I BELIEVE YOU
WOULD TELL ME TO
_____

I'M AFRAID THAT
_____

THREE THINGS I NEED TO GET
DONE (E.G., CALL ABOUT SS
BENEFITS)
_____

I WILL ASK THESE PEOPLE FOR
HELP TODAY
_____

THOUGHT FOR THE WEEK
_____

*"WHEN THE LORD SAW HER, HIS
HEART OVERFLOWED WITH
COMPASSION. "DON'T CRY! HE SAID"
(LUKE 7:13 NLV)*

# Evening check in

AT THIS MOMENT, I FEEL

THE HARDEST TIME OF THE DAY
TODAY WAS
_____

I THOUGHT OF YOU  TODAY WHEN
_____

MY GREATEST TRIGGER TODAY
WAS
_____

I FOUND HOPE TODAY WHEN
_____

IF I COULD TALK TO YOU RIGHT
NOW, I WOULD TELL YOU
_____

I CELEBRATED YOU TODAY BY

### *Prompts for writing a love letter to your spouse*

You've made it through another week. I hope this week was a little easier for you. Did you experience any anxious moments? What did you do to get through it? Did it help?

It's that time again. Continue to use your thoughts from the daily check-ins to write your letter. Some of the weekly prompts are below:

- This week, my biggest fear was.......
- The most difficult time of the day for me this week was......
- I thought of you when........
- My fondest memory of you this week was......
- I got these things done this week....
- I found hope this week when.....
- If I could talk to you right now, I would tell you....
- I believe you would tell me to.....

Otherwise, write what feels right to you. It's up to you.

Date _____

*Dear*

_____
_____
_____
_____
_____
_____
_____
_____
_____
_____
_____
_____
_____
_____
_____
_____
_____
_____
_____
_____
_____

## *A Photographic Tribute To Your Spouse*

Choose another picture or create a collage of pictures you believe can give you a sense of peace for the week ahead.

# Week 4

# Hope

"Hope is being able to see that there is light despite all of the darkness." ~ Desmond Tutu

**_Thought for the week:_**

"Hope is being able to see that there is light despite all of the darkness." ~ Desmond Tutu

Sometimes it's the little things that give you hope during this grief journey. MY mother-in-law gave me a snow globe with a cardinal (red bird) just before the Christmas holidays. The belief is that when someone passes, the presence of a cardinal is a reminder that the person is near. She shared that she had been seeing a cardinal perched on her kitchen window as she washed dishes. I had never thought about it before, but I got really excited when I saw a cardinal in my backyard, just chilling on the patio. Then, it seemed to 'visit' more frequently. I recently moved away from the town where I met and shared my life with my husband so that I could be closer to our daughter's family. After completing some yard work, I noticed a cardinal hanging around the area as if it was inspecting my work. It made me chuckle because I often called him my supervisor. I sent a text message to my daughter musing that my husband was inspecting my handiwork. He was the yardman of the family. I had never mowed the lawn before. As a matter of fact, I had to ask my dad to show me how to turn the mower on.

Although I have amazing friends who became like family, I knew I needed the comfort of being with my daughter and her family. My husband and I had already discussed moving near the grandkids when we retired, so my decision to move was not a difficult one. In fact, when I told my supervisor about my plans, she advised that she knew I would make that decision at some point. Being able to closely watch my grandkids grow as well as having the opportunity to share in little experiences with them, such as picking them up from school when needed gives me hope that it's going to eventually be ok.

I know this might be difficult but think of what HOPE could look like for you at some point in time. For me, it is my grandkids, but what do you think will bring you joy in the future?

The reality is that our spouses are not coming back in their physical form. Maybe the thought of your spouse watching over you makes you feel hopeful. Maybe, you now have an opportunity to do something you dreamed of doing, and that gives you hope. Remember, this is your journey. It's new territory for you. Find whatever will give you a feeling of hope and when you feel yourself slipping, hold onto that.

# Morning check in

DATE _____

AT THIS MOMENT, I FEEL

ONE THING I CAN DO TO GET THROUGH THE DAY

○ _____

THE MEMORY I WILL FOCUS ON TODAY IS
_____

IF YOU WERE HERE, I BELIEVE YOU WOULD TELL ME TO
_____

I'M AFRAID THAT
_____

THREE THINGS I NEED TO GET DONE (E.G., CALL ABOUT SS BENEFITS)
_____

I WILL ASK THESE PEOPLE FOR HELP TODAY
_____

THOUGHT FOR THE WEEK
_____

*"WHEN THE LORD SAW HER, HIS HEART OVERFLOWED WITH COMPASSION. "DON'T CRY! HE SAID" (LUKE 7:13 NLV)*

# Evening check in

AT THIS MOMENT, I FEEL

THE HARDEST TIME OF THE DAY
TODAY WAS

I THOUGHT OF YOU  TODAY WHEN

MY GREATEST TRIGGER TODAY
WAS

I FOUND HOPE TODAY WHEN

IF I COULD TALK TO YOU RIGHT
NOW, I WOULD TELL YOU

I CELEBRATED YOU TODAY BY

# Morning check in

DATE _____

AT THIS MOMENT, I FEEL

ONE THING I CAN DO TO GET THROUGH THE DAY

○ _____

THE MEMORY I WILL FOCUS ON TODAY IS
_____

IF YOU WERE HERE, I BELIEVE YOU WOULD TELL ME TO
_____

I'M AFRAID THAT
_____

THREE THINGS I NEED TO GET DONE (E.G., CALL ABOUT SS BENEFITS)
_____

I WILL ASK THESE PEOPLE FOR HELP TODAY
_____

THOUGHT FOR THE WEEK
_____

*"WHEN THE LORD SAW HER, HIS HEART OVERFLOWED WITH COMPASSION. "DON'T CRY! HE SAID" (LUKE 7:13 NLV)*

# Evening check in

AT THIS MOMENT, I FEEL

I THOUGHT OF YOU  TODAY WHEN

I FOUND HOPE TODAY WHEN

I CELEBRATED YOU TODAY BY

THE HARDEST TIME OF THE DAY TODAY WAS

MY GREATEST TRIGGER TODAY WAS

IF I COULD TALK TO YOU RIGHT NOW, I WOULD TELL YOU

# Morning check in

DATE _____

AT THIS MOMENT, I FEEL

I'M AFRAID THAT
_____

THREE THINGS I NEED TO GET
DONE (E.G., CALL ABOUT SS
BENEFITS)
_____

ONE THING I CAN DO TO GET
THROUGH THE DAY

○ _____

THE MEMORY I WILL FOCUS ON
TODAY IS
_____

I WILL ASK THESE PEOPLE FOR
HELP TODAY
_____

IF YOU WERE HERE, I BELIEVE YOU
WOULD TELL ME TO
_____

THOUGHT FOR THE WEEK
_____

*"WHEN THE LORD SAW HER, HIS
HEART OVERFLOWED WITH
COMPASSION. "DON'T CRY! HE SAID"
(LUKE 7:13 NLV)*

# Evening check in

AT THIS MOMENT, I FEEL

THE HARDEST TIME OF THE DAY
TODAY WAS
_____

I THOUGHT OF YOU  TODAY WHEN
_____

MY GREATEST TRIGGER TODAY
WAS
_____

I FOUND HOPE TODAY WHEN
_____

IF I COULD TALK TO YOU RIGHT
NOW, I WOULD TELL YOU
_____

I CELEBRATED YOU TODAY BY

# Morning check in

DATE _____

AT THIS MOMENT, I FEEL

I'M AFRAID THAT
_____

ONE THING I CAN DO TO GET
THROUGH THE DAY

○ _____

THREE THINGS I NEED TO GET
DONE (E.G., CALL ABOUT SS
BENEFITS)
_____

THE MEMORY I WILL FOCUS ON
TODAY IS
_____

I WILL ASK THESE PEOPLE FOR
HELP TODAY
_____

IF YOU WERE HERE, I BELIEVE YOU
WOULD TELL ME TO
_____

THOUGHT FOR THE WEEK
_____

*"WHEN THE LORD SAW HER, HIS
HEART OVERFLOWED WITH
COMPASSION. "DON'T CRY! HE SAID"
(LUKE 7:13 NLV)*

# Evening check in

AT THIS MOMENT, I FEEL

THE HARDEST TIME OF THE DAY
TODAY WAS

I THOUGHT OF YOU  TODAY WHEN

MY GREATEST TRIGGER TODAY
WAS

I FOUND HOPE TODAY WHEN

IF I COULD TALK TO YOU RIGHT
NOW, I WOULD TELL YOU

I CELEBRATED YOU TODAY BY

# Morning check in

DATE _____

AT THIS MOMENT, I FEEL

ONE THING I CAN DO TO GET
THROUGH THE DAY

○ _____

THE MEMORY I WILL FOCUS ON
TODAY IS

_____

IF YOU WERE HERE, I BELIEVE YOU
WOULD TELL ME TO

_____

I'M AFRAID THAT

_____

THREE THINGS I NEED TO GET
DONE (E.G., CALL ABOUT SS
BENEFITS)

_____

I WILL ASK THESE PEOPLE FOR
HELP TODAY

_____

THOUGHT FOR THE WEEK

_____

*"WHEN THE LORD SAW HER, HIS
HEART OVERFLOWED WITH
COMPASSION. "DON'T CRY! HE SAID"
(LUKE 7:13 NLV)*

# Evening check in

AT THIS MOMENT, I FEEL

I THOUGHT OF YOU  TODAY WHEN

I FOUND HOPE TODAY WHEN

I CELEBRATED YOU TODAY BY

THE HARDEST TIME OF THE DAY
TODAY WAS

MY GREATEST TRIGGER TODAY
WAS

IF I COULD TALK TO YOU RIGHT
NOW, I WOULD TELL YOU

# Morning check in

DATE _____

AT THIS MOMENT, I FEEL

ONE THING I CAN DO TO GET
THROUGH THE DAY

○ _____

THE MEMORY I WILL FOCUS ON
TODAY IS
_____

IF YOU WERE HERE, I BELIEVE YOU
WOULD TELL ME TO
_____

I'M AFRAID THAT
_____

THREE THINGS I NEED TO GET
DONE (E.G., CALL ABOUT SS
BENEFITS)
_____

I WILL ASK THESE PEOPLE FOR
HELP TODAY
_____

THOUGHT FOR THE WEEK
_____

*"WHEN THE LORD SAW HER, HIS
HEART OVERFLOWED WITH
COMPASSION. "DON'T CRY! HE SAID"
(LUKE 7:13 NLV)*

# Evening check in

AT THIS MOMENT, I FEEL

I THOUGHT OF YOU  TODAY WHEN
_____

I FOUND HOPE TODAY WHEN
_____

I CELEBRATED YOU TODAY BY

THE HARDEST TIME OF THE DAY
TODAY WAS
_____

MY GREATEST TRIGGER TODAY
WAS
_____

IF I COULD TALK TO YOU RIGHT
NOW, I WOULD TELL YOU
_____

# Morning check in

DATE _____

AT THIS MOMENT, I FEEL

I'M AFRAID THAT
_____

ONE THING I CAN DO TO GET
THROUGH THE DAY

○ _____

THREE THINGS I NEED TO GET
DONE (E.G., CALL ABOUT SS
BENEFITS)
_____

THE MEMORY I WILL FOCUS ON
TODAY IS
_____

I WILL ASK THESE PEOPLE FOR
HELP TODAY
_____

IF YOU WERE HERE, I BELIEVE YOU
WOULD TELL ME TO
_____

THOUGHT FOR THE WEEK
_____

*"WHEN THE LORD SAW HER, HIS
HEART OVERFLOWED WITH
COMPASSION. "DON'T CRY! HE SAID"
(LUKE 7:13 NLV)*

# Evening check in

AT THIS MOMENT, I FEEL

I THOUGHT OF YOU  TODAY WHEN

I FOUND HOPE TODAY WHEN

I CELEBRATED YOU TODAY BY

THE HARDEST TIME OF THE DAY
TODAY WAS

MY GREATEST TRIGGER TODAY
WAS

IF I COULD TALK TO YOU RIGHT
NOW, I WOULD TELL YOU

### *Prompts for writing a love letter to your spouse*

This is it,! You've made it through the last 28 days! How do you feel? Are you still overwhelmed? I'm quite sure you are still sad and it's possible that you are still anxious about this grief journey. I won't lie to you. I don't think it will ever be easy. I don't think the grief ever fully goes away. You just learn how to cope with it to make your life a little easier.

It is time to write your final letter. Again, don't overthink it. You can continue using the prompts below, or you can throw caution to the wind and write whatever remains on your heart to share at this moment. It is truly up to you, so go for it.

- This week, my biggest fear was.......
- The most difficult time of the day for me this week was......
- I thought of you when........
- My fondest memory of you this week was......
- I got these things done this week....
- I found hope this week when.....
- If I could talk to you right now, I would tell you....
- I believe you would tell me to.....

Date _____

*Dear*

_____

_____

_____

_____

_____

_____

_____

_____

_____

_____

_____

_____

_____

_____

_____

_____

## A Photographic Tribute To Your Spouse

Choose another picture or create a collage of pictures you believe can give you hope for the week ahead.

# Final Thought

Congratulations! You've made it through the first 28 days of your grief journey. I know it doesn't feel like time for celebrating but you've accomplished a great feat towards your healing. The days ahead won't be easy, but hopefully you can take something you've learned from the past 28 days with you.

In my opinion, this first year is a roller coaster of emotions. There are so many 'firsts' that you'll experience alone - birthdays, anniversaries, and special holidays. My husband and I were not big Valentine's Day people. We didn't make a big deal of it. Since we usually cooked dinner at nights, we just planned something a little fancier. Because of this, I thought I would be ok on the first Valentine's Day without him. Boy was I wrong! I got ready for work that morning, got in my car, pulled out of the garage, and sat in my driveway crying - I mean the 'ugly cry'. Needless to say, I didn't go to work that day. A friend checked in on me at some point and I shared that I was having a rough day. She invited me for a mani-pedi that afternoon. This was exactly what I needed to get through the day.

My family and friends have been with me throughout this journey. I've also had two friends whose husbands passed away around the same time. We try to encourage each other, which I believe serves to encourage ourselves. I strongly suggest that you lean on your support system as much as you can. Be honest with yourself and with others. This isn't the time to 'fake it till you make it". Now, I'm not saying to walk around all day telling everyone how you really feel, but I'm saying that you'll know who to share your true emotions with. When someone asks me how I am doing, if it's a good day, I tell them that. If it's not a good day and the person is someone I don't mind sharing with, I say it's not a good day and I might elaborate. If I am not in the mood to go deeper into the conversation I usually say something like, I'm taking it day-by-day, or I'm getting through the day. Most people won't press.

I want to remind you though, that it is difficult to go through the grieving process alone. Yes, you need to be strong for you and your kids, if you have kids. You don't have to show a brave face all of the time though. If you have kids, they are grieving their loss as well and they need to learn how to do that in a healthy way. It's ok to cry in front of them. It's ok to cry with them. Honestly, it's ok to cry wherever and whenever. Let it out. If you bottle it up, you are going to explode like a can of soda that was shaken and then opened. You will meltdown at the most inconvenient times. However, if you allow yourself the grace to work through your emotions, you will be able to control it a little better. I recognized that I was very emotional in the mornings when I got out of bed. That was my time. For a while though, when the tears came, I quickly jumped out of bed and started taking care of my morning duties. My counselor suggested that I schedule a time each morning before I got out of bed to cry. If I chose for it to be five minutes, I needed to sit through the emotions for five minutes and allow it to play out without trying to fill that space with something else to avoid it. Sometimes I talked to him. Other times, I just cried. I can honestly say that this has helped me tremendously.

If you have not started speaking with a counselor, I encourage you to look for one. Thankfully, it is becoming less taboo for us as black women to seek counseling to help us cope with the challenges life brings. I promise you that you cannot depend on your family and friends for this. If they haven't dealt with the loss of a spouse it is difficult for them to truly understand your grief. Since I was already going to a regular counselor, I continued with her and I believe she was extremely helpful. Some would suggest that you need a grief counselor. I believe it's your choice and you have the ability to shop around to find the right fit for you. There are a variety of options available. Maybe you are a member of a church that offers counseling, or your job provides an employee assistance program. Maybe there is a local grief group in your community that meets regularly. My husband was under hospice care for a week. They offered virtual grief groups.

I was invited by a friend to a 6-week mourners program at her church. It helped to be around others who were at different stages of their grief journey. It was truly a learning experience. Your health insurance may also provide opportunities for counseling. Find out what your options are and go from there.

As you go on with your life (however that looks for you), I wish you comfort, strength, peace and hope. You'll get through this eventually. Take it one moment at a time. Obviously you will cry a lot, but also find ways to reflect on the good times with your spouse. Those great memories will carry you through. I hope that you'll laugh a little. I don't know the exact science around laughter, but I know that it helps. All the best.......

## *A Photographic Tribute To Your Spouse*

For the final project, I thought it would be fitting to have you select a few different pictures to create a collage. The first picture should be of you smiling or laughing. You can use one with you alone, or with your spouse, kids or girlfriend(s). The second picture should be of you doing something you enjoyed e.g., dancing, singing, traveling, whatever. Then, choose another picture you believe would help you to not give up on yourself. When it gets tough (there will be some tough days ahead), you will have something to motivate you to go on.

Made in the USA
Columbia, SC
21 October 2022